In Honor of the expected arrival of

_____

Date

_____

Guests

Name and Relationship to the Parents

_____
_____

Advice for Parentes

_____
_____
_____

Wishes for Baby

_____
_____
_____

Guests

Name and Relationship to the Parents

_____
_____

Advice for Parentes

_____
_____
_____
_____

Wishes for Baby

_____
_____
_____

Guests

Name and Relationship to the Parents

_____
_____

Advice for Parentes

_____
_____
_____
_____

Wishes for Baby

_____
_____
_____

Guests

Name and Relationship to the Parents

_____
_____

Advice for Parentes

_____
_____
_____
_____

Wishes for Baby

_____
_____
_____

Guests

Name and Relationship to the Parents

_____

_____

Advice for Parents

_____

_____

_____

Wishes for Baby

_____

_____

_____

Guests

Name and Relationship to the Parents

_____

_____

Advice for Parentes

_____

_____

_____

_____

Wishes for Baby

_____

_____

_____

Guests

Name and Relationship to the Parents

_____

_____

Advice for Parentes

_____

_____

_____

Wishes for Baby

_____

_____

_____

Guests

Name and Relationship to the Parents

_____

_____

Advice for Parentes

_____

_____

_____

_____

Wishes for Baby

_____

_____

_____

Guests

Name and Relationship to the Parents

_____

_____

Advice for Parentes

_____

_____

_____

Wishes for Baby

_____

_____

_____

Guests

Name and Relationship to the Parents

_____
_____

Advice for Parentes

_____
_____
_____

Wishes for Baby

_____
_____
_____

Guests

Name and Relationship to the Parents

Advice for Parentes

Wishes for Baby

Guests

Name and Relationship to the Parents

_____

_____

Advice for Parentes

_____

_____

_____

Wishes for Baby

_____

_____

_____

Guests

Name and Relationship to the Parents

_____

_____

Advice for Parentes

_____

_____

_____

Wishes for Baby

_____

_____

_____

Guests

Name and Relationship to the Parents

_____

_____

Advice for Parentes

_____

_____

_____

Wishes for Baby

_____

_____

_____

Guests

Name and Relationship to the Parents

_____

_____

Advice for Parentes

_____

_____

_____

Wishes for Baby

_____

_____

_____

Guests

Name and Relationship to the Parents

_____

_____

Advice for Parentes

_____

_____

_____

_____

Wishes for Baby

_____

_____

_____

Guests

Name and Relationship to the Parents

_____
_____

Advice for Parentes

_____
_____
_____
_____

Wishes for Baby

_____
_____
_____

Guests

Name and Relationship to the Parents

_____

_____

Advice for Parentes

_____

_____

_____

Wishes for Baby

_____

_____

_____

Guests

Name and Relationship to the Parents

_____

_____

Advice for Parentes

_____

_____

_____

Wishes for Baby

_____

_____

_____

Guests

Name and Relationship to the Parents

_____

_____

Advice for Parentes

_____

_____

_____

Wishes for Baby

_____

_____

_____

Guests

Name and Relationship to the Parents

_____

_____

Advice for Parentes

_____

_____

_____

_____

Wishes for Baby

_____

_____

_____

Guests

Name and Relationship to the Parents

_____

_____

Advice for Parentes

_____

_____

_____

Wishes for Baby

_____

_____

_____

Guests

Name and Relationship to the Parents

_____

_____

Advice for Parentes

_____

_____

_____

Wishes for Baby

_____

_____

_____

Guests

Name and Relationship to the Parents

_____
_____

Advice for Parentes

_____
_____
_____

Wishes for Baby

_____
_____
_____

Guests

Name and Relationship to the Parents

Advice for Parentes

Wishes for Baby

Guests

Name and Relationship to the Parents

___

___

Advice for Parents

___

___

___

Wishes for Baby

___

___

___

Guests

Name and Relationship to the Parents

Advice for Parentes

Wishes for Baby

Guests

Name and Relationship to the Parents

_____

_____

Advice for Parentes

_____

_____

_____

Wishes for Baby

_____

_____

_____

Guests

Name and Relationship to the Parents

_____

_____

Advice for Parentes

_____

_____

_____

Wishes for Baby

_____

_____

_____

Guests

Name and Relationship to the Parents

_____

_____

Advice for Parents

_____

_____

_____

Wishes for Baby

_____

_____

_____

Guests

Name and Relationship to the Parents

_____

_____

Advice for Parentes

_____

_____

_____

_____

Wishes for Baby

_____

_____

_____

Guests

Name and Relationship to the Parents

_____
_____

Advice for Parentes

_____
_____
_____

Wishes for Baby

_____
_____
_____

Guests

Name and Relationship to the Parents

_____

_____

Advice for Parentes

_____

_____

_____

Wishes for Baby

_____

_____

_____

Guests

Name and Relationship to the Parents

_____

_____

Advice for Parentes

_____

_____

_____

_____

Wishes for Baby

_____

_____

_____

Guests

Name and Relationship to the Parents

_____

_____

Advice for Parentes

_____

_____

_____

Wishes for Baby

_____

_____

_____

Guests

Name and Relationship to the Parents

_____
_____

Advice for Parentes

_____
_____
_____
_____

Wishes for Baby

_____
_____
_____

Guests

Name and Relationship to the Parents

_____

_____

Advice for Parentes

_____

_____

_____

Wishes for Baby

_____

_____

_____

Guests

Name and Relationship to the Parents

_____

_____

Advice for Parentes

_____

_____

_____

Wishes for Baby

_____

_____

_____

Guests

Name and Relationship to the Parents

_____

_____

Advice for Parentes

_____

_____

_____

Wishes for Baby

_____

_____

_____

Guests

Name and Relationship to the Parents

_____
_____

Advice for Parentes

_____
_____
_____

Wishes for Baby

_____
_____
_____

Guests

Name and Relationship to the Parents

_____

_____

Advice for Parentes

_____

_____

_____

Wishes for Baby

_____

_____

_____

Guests

Name and Relationship to the Parents

_____

_____

Advice for Parentes

_____

_____

_____

_____

Wishes for Baby

_____

_____

_____

Guests

Name and Relationship to the Parents

_____

_____

Advice for Parents

_____

_____

_____

_____

Wishes for Baby

_____

_____

_____

Guests

Name and Relationship to the Parents

_____
_____

Advice for Parentes

_____
_____
_____
_____

Wishes for Baby

_____
_____
_____
_____

Guests

Name and Relationship to the Parents

_____

_____

Advice for Parentes

_____

_____

_____

Wishes for Baby

_____

_____

_____

Guests

Name and Relationship to the Parents

_____
_____

Advice for Parentes

_____
_____
_____
_____

Wishes for Baby

_____
_____
_____

Guests

Name and Relationship to the Parents

Advice for Parentes

Wishes for Baby

Guests

Name and Relationship to the Parents

_____

_____

Advice for Parentes

_____

_____

_____

Wishes for Baby

_____

_____

_____

Guests

Name and Relationship to the Parents

_____

_____

Advice for Parentes

_____

_____

_____

Wishes for Baby

_____

_____

_____

Guests

Name and Relationship to the Parents

_____

_____

Advice for Parentes

_____

_____

_____

Wishes for Baby

_____

_____

_____

Guests

Name and Relationship to the Parents

_____

_____

Advice for Parentes

_____

_____

_____

Wishes for Baby

_____

_____

_____

Guests

Name and Relationship to the Parents

_____

_____

Advice for Parentes

_____

_____

_____

_____

Wishes for Baby

_____

_____

_____

Guests

Name and Relationship to the Parents

_____

_____

Advice for Parentes

_____

_____

_____

Wishes for Baby

_____

_____

_____

Guests

Name and Relationship to the Parents

_____

_____

Advice for Parents

_____

_____

_____

_____

Wishes for Baby

_____

_____

_____

Guests

Name and Relationship to the Parents

_____

_____

Advice for Parentes

_____

_____

_____

_____

Wishes for Baby

_____

_____

_____

Guests

Name and Relationship to the Parents

_____
_____

Advice for Parentes

_____
_____
_____
_____

Wishes for Baby

_____
_____
_____

Guests

Name and Relationship to the Parents

_____
_____

Advice for Parentes

_____
_____
_____
_____

Wishes for Baby

_____
_____
_____

Guests

Name and Relationship to the Parents

_____

_____

Advice for Parentes

_____

_____

_____

Wishes for Baby

_____

_____

_____

Guests

Name and Relationship to the Parents

_____

_____

Advice for Parentes

_____

_____

_____

Wishes for Baby

_____

_____

_____

Guests

Name and Relationship to the Parents

_____

_____

Advice for Parentes

_____

_____

_____

_____

Wishes for Baby

_____

_____

_____

Guests

Name and Relationship to the Parents

_____

_____

Advice for Parentes

_____

_____

_____

_____

Wishes for Baby

_____

_____

_____

Guests

Name and Relationship to the Parents

_____

_____

Advice for Parentes

_____

_____

_____

_____

Wishes for Baby

_____

_____

_____

Guests

Name and Relationship to the Parents

_____

_____

Advice for Parentes

_____

_____

_____

Wishes for Baby

_____

_____

_____

Guests

Name and Relationship to the Parents

_____

_____

Advice for Parentes

_____

_____

_____

Wishes for Baby

_____

_____

_____

Guests

Name and Relationship to the Parents

Advice for Parentes

Wishes for Baby

Guests

Name and Relationship to the Parents

_____
_____

Advice for Parentes

_____
_____
_____

Wishes for Baby

_____
_____
_____

Guests

Name and Relationship to the Parents

_____

_____

Advice for Parentes

_____

_____

_____

Wishes for Baby

_____

_____

_____

Guests

Name and Relationship to the Parents

_____

_____

Advice for Parentes

_____

_____

_____

Wishes for Baby

_____

_____

_____

Guests

Name and Relationship to the Parents

_____

_____

Advice for Parentes

_____

_____

_____

_____

Wishes for Baby

_____

_____

_____

Guests

Name and Relationship to the Parents

_____

_____

Advice for Parentes

_____

_____

_____

Wishes for Baby

_____

_____

_____

Guests

Name and Relationship to the Parents

_____

_____

Advice for Parentes

_____

_____

_____

Wishes for Baby

_____

_____

_____

Guests

Name and Relationship to the Parents

_____

_____

Advice for Parentes

_____

_____

_____

_____

Wishes for Baby

_____

_____

_____

Guests

Name and Relationship to the Parents

_____
_____

Advice for Parentes

_____
_____
_____
_____

Wishes for Baby

_____
_____
_____

Guests

Name and Relationship to the Parents

_____
_____

Advice for Parentes

_____
_____
_____
_____

Wishes for Baby

_____
_____
_____

Guests

Name and Relationship to the Parents

_____

_____

Advice for Parentes

_____

_____

_____

_____

Wishes for Baby

_____

_____

_____

Guests

Name and Relationship to the Parents

_____

_____

Advice for Parentes

_____

_____

_____

_____

Wishes for Baby

_____

_____

_____

Guests

Name and Relationship to the Parents

___

Advice for Parentes

___

Wishes for Baby

___

Guests

Name and Relationship to the Parents

_____

_____

Advice for Parentes

_____

_____

_____

Wishes for Baby

_____

_____

_____

Guests

Name and Relationship to the Parents

_____
_____

Advice for Parentes

_____
_____
_____
_____

Wishes for Baby

_____
_____
_____

Guests

Name and Relationship to the Parents

_____

_____

Advice for Parentes

_____

_____

_____

Wishes for Baby

_____

_____

_____

Guests

Name and Relationship to the Parents

Advice for Parentes

Wishes for Baby

Guests

Name and Relationship to the Parents

_____

_____

Advice for Parentes

_____

_____

_____

_____

Wishes for Baby

_____

_____

_____

Guests

Name and Relationship to the Parents

_____

_____

Advice for Parentes

_____

_____

_____

_____

Wishes for Baby

_____

_____

_____

Guests

Name and Relationship to the Parents

_____

_____

Advice for Parentes

_____

_____

_____

Wishes for Baby

_____

_____

_____

Guests

Name and Relationship to the Parents

_____

_____

Advice for Parentes

_____

_____

_____

Wishes for Baby

_____

_____

_____

Guests

Name and Relationship to the Parents

_____

_____

Advice for Parentes

_____

_____

_____

Wishes for Baby

_____

_____

_____

Guests

Name and Relationship to the Parents

_____

_____

Advice for Parentes

_____

_____

_____

Wishes for Baby

_____

_____

_____

Guests

Name and Relationship to the Parents

_____
_____

Advice for Parentes

_____
_____
_____

Wishes for Baby

_____
_____
_____

Guests

Name and Relationship to the Parents

___

___

Advice for Parentes

___

___

___

Wishes for Baby

___

___

___

Guests

Name and Relationship to the Parents

_____

_____

Advice for Parentes

_____

_____

_____

_____

Wishes for Baby

_____

_____

_____

Gift Log

Given By	Gift(s) Received

Gift Log

Given By	Gift(s) Received

Gift Log

Given By   **Gift(s) Received**

Gift Log

Given By | **Gift(s) Received**

Gift Log

Given By   **Gift(s) Received**

Given By	Gift(s) Received

Gift Log

Given By   **Gift(s) Received**

Gift Log

Given By   **Gift(s) Received**

Gift Log

Given By   **Gift(s) Received**

Gift Log

Given By	Gift(s) Received

Gift Log

Given By　　　　　　　　　　　　　　　**Gift(s) Received**

Made in the USA
Columbia, SC
16 March 2025